GREEN RIVER

Anglers heaven at lunker flats. You can almost count spots on these trout in four feet of water. The fish are used to anglers and bad presentations. Your presentation must be accurate and natural.

GREEN RIVER

Larry Tullis

Photographs by the author

Fly plates photographed by Jim Schollmeyer

Frank
Amato

PORTLAND

River Journal

Volume 1, Number 3, 1993

About The Author

Larry Tullis is a freelance writer who lives in Orem, Utah, when in town. He has spent about 1000 days on the Green River fishing and guiding and enjoys sharing what he has learned with others interested in this remarkable fishery. His writing, photography and illustrations have been published in Flyfishing, Fly Fishermen, Flyfisher, Fly Fishing News, Outdoor Photographer, Utah Fishing, Sports Guide, Idaho Wildlife, Trout (Stackpole book), Anglers Sport Calenders etc. and a forthcoming book "Small Flies For Trout" will be published by Odysseus Editions (Lefty's Little Library Of Fly Fishing) in early 1994. He is an associate producer of the Outdoor World and Inside Outdoors TV shows and travels the fishing globe when he can, fishing for anything that will hit a fly. He currently guides in Alaska in the summer. Larry has guided on the Green River for a number of years and on the Henry's Fork in Idaho previous to that. Mr. Tullis is the originator of the Wiggle Bug fly series, does slide shows, technique seminars and is a consultant to several fishing equipment manufacturers. He is single and probably will be until he finds a gal who will put up with all his fishing. Besides being a fly fishing pro, he enjoys backpacking, X-country skiing, art, photography, watercraft sports, good fishing, good entertainment and good friends.

◆

Foreword

The Green River has been a special place for me. It has been a companion, a friend and a teacher. The friends I've made and the things I've experienced there are among my most valued possessions. This book was difficult to write only because I was limited on the length. It could have easily been twice as long but I hope the information provided will give you an idea of what this area is like and how to fish the waters of the Green River. I've been wanting to write about the Green for some time but the fishery has been going through many changes in the last few years and is just starting to reach a balance. The future outlook is good thanks to a core of concerned anglers and informed management. Without the efforts of the Green River guides and fishery biologists, the river would not be what it is today, a world class fishery that attracts people from all over the world.

◆

Series Editor: Frank Amato

Subscriptions:
Softbound: $30.00 for one year (four issues)
$55.00 for two years
Hardbound Limited Editions: $80.00 one year, $150.00 for two years.

Design: Joyce Herbst
Cover Photography: Larry Tullis
Fly Plate Photography: Jim Schollmeyer • Map: Tony Amato
Printed in Hong Kong
Softbound ISBN: 1-878175-45-9   Hardbound ISBN: 1-878175-46-7

(Hardbound Edition Limited To 500 Copies)

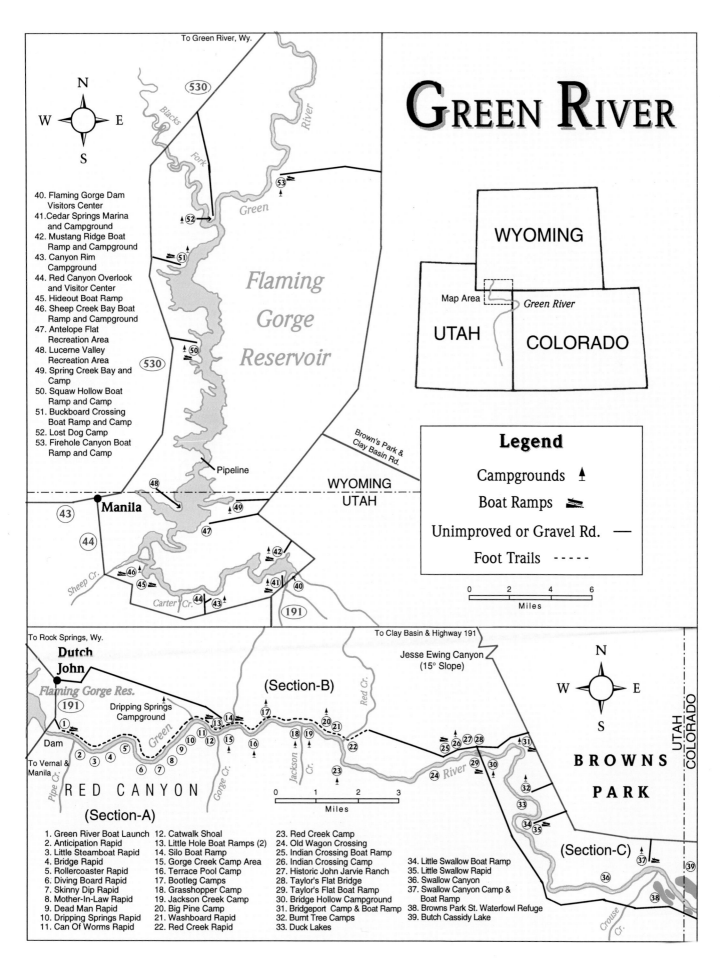

GREEN RIVER

N W E S

WYOMING

UTAH   COLORADO

Map Area   *Green River*

40. Flaming Gorge Dam Visitors Center
41. Cedar Springs Marina and Campground
42. Mustang Ridge Boat Ramp and Campground
43. Canyon Rim Campground
44. Red Canyon Overlook and Visitor Center
45. Hideout Boat Ramp
46. Sheep Creek Bay Boat Ramp and Campground
47. Antelope Flat Recreation Area
48. Lucerne Valley Recreation Area
49. Spring Creek Bay and Camp
50. Squaw Hollow Boat Ramp and Camp
51. Buckboard Crossing Boat Ramp and Camp
52. Lost Dog Camp
53. Firehole Canyon Boat Ramp and Camp

Flaming Gorge Reservoir

To Green River, Wy.
530

Blacks Fork

Green River

Pipeline

Manila

WYOMING
UTAH

Brown's Park & Clay Basin Rd.

Sheep Cr.

Carter Cr.

191

Legend

Campgrounds ▲
Boat Ramps ⛴
Unimproved or Gravel Rd. —
Foot Trails - - - - -

0   2   4   6
Miles

To Rock Springs, Wy.

Dutch John

Flaming Gorge Res.
191

Dripping Springs Campground

To Vernal & Manila

Dam

R E D   C A N Y O N

(Section-A)

To Clay Basin & Highway 191

Jesse Ewing Canyon (15° Slope)

(Section-B)

Red Cr.

Green

Gorge Cr.

Jackson Cr.

N W E S

B R O W N S
P A R K

UTAH
COLORADO

River

(Section-C)

Crouse Cr.

0   1   2   3
Miles

1. Green River Boat Launch
2. Anticipation Rapid
3. Little Steamboat Rapid
4. Bridge Rapid
5. Rollercoaster Rapid
6. Diving Board Rapid
7. Skinny Dip Rapid
8. Mother-In-Law Rapid
9. Dead Man Rapid
10. Dripping Springs Rapid
11. Can Of Worms Rapid

12. Catwalk Shoal
13. Little Hole Boat Ramps (2)
14. Silo Boat Ramp
15. Gorge Creek Camp Area
16. Terrace Pool Camp
17. Bootleg Camps
18. Grasshopper Camp
19. Jackson Creek Camp
20. Big Pine Camp
21. Washboard Rapid
22. Red Creek Rapid

23. Red Creek Camp
24. Old Wagon Crossing
25. Indian Crossing Boat Ramp
26. Indian Crossing Camp
27. Historic John Jarvie Ranch
28. Taylor's Flat Bridge
29. Taylor's Flat Boat Ramp
30. Bridge Hollow Campground
31. Bridgeport Camp & Boat Ramp
32. Burnt Tree Camps
33. Duck Lakes

34. Little Swallow Boat Ramp
35. Little Swallow Rapid
36. Swallow Canyon
37. Swallow Canyon Camp & Boat Ramp
38. Browns Park St. Waterfowl Refuge
39. Butch Cassidy Lake

The clear waters, red rock canyon and coniferous slopes of ponderosa pine, pinion poine, white pine and juniper combine to make a unique and awe inspiring fishing experience. A dory nears the end of Red Canyon.

GREEN RIVER

◆

THE OLIVE SCUD IMITATION DRIFTED DEEP IN the run below Deadman Rapids on the Green River. The fly line began to belly so it was mended carefully and more slack introduced for a long drift. Above the green ribbon of water, red canyon walls rose to a deep azure blue sky, despite the brief thunder shower just half an hour ago. The air was crystalline and heavy with the scent of drying pine, sage and grasses. A breeze rustled through the needles of the shoreline Ponderosa pines, barely heard over the sound of water, but somehow soothing. The cool water swirled around legs devoid of waders, the warming air and sun compensating nicely for 48 degree water. Most of the surroundings were subconsciously logged as full concentration narrowed down to the drift at hand.

Ever so slightly did the strike indicator hesitate and begin to slide underwater. The rod hand automatically rose and the deep bend indicated contact with something. A brief pause determined a pulse of life on the other end, not the static feel of a rock. Time stood still.

The fish shook it's head and flared it's gills, trying to dislodge the scud that had bit back. The rod throbbed several times, then the reel began to sing as the fish shot up and across the river, covering 75 feet in half a breath, then vault-

ing into the air, spraying thousands of diamonds embedded in sunlight, revealing it to be a very large cuttbow hybrid, well over 10 pounds. The instant of re-entry triggered a downstream run that took it on the other side of a large boulder. A lucky roll cast and some slack line allowed the current to wash the line free of the rock. Some slack line was retrieved, but only for a second as the fish freight trained downstream for some unseen destination.

With heart pounding fast as the revolutions of the reel showed line melting off the reel, the angler stumbled downstream to chase the fish. A dropoff required the angler to get on shore to continue downstream after the silver bullet. A brief glance showed that the end of the fly line was out so far that only backing showed and the fish must already be in the next rapids. There was a sudden release of pressure and a few strips of line confirmed that the fish was gone.

A brief letdown was followed by a grin and a chuckle. Again, the biggest fish I'd ever hooked got away. Maybe next time. That fish has never left me. It's etched in the spot where my fondest memories reside.

The Green River is one of those places that can get into your soul. It's a relationship that can become a part of who you are. Since humanity left life as hunter-gatherers and turned to communities or what some call "civilization," we have also felt the need to turn back to seek refuge in nature. Many seem compelled to seek out the sensations of our primordial heritage, which seems to awaken senses that are dormant or dulled by our civilized existence.

The Green River, from it's majestic, yet humble beginnings in the Wind River Mountains to it's confluence with the mighty Colorado River, is still a beautiful, inviting slice of nature. It's largely unsettled territory and wealth of natural resources beckon to those who know of it's timeless qualities.

Mountain men of the 1800's and characters of the old west were drawn to the Green River country and legends from that era still abound. Jim Bridger called this area home base for a time and Butch Cassidy and the Wild Bunch often retreated here to escape pressure from the law.

Today, it is an anglers paradise, drawing fishermen from all over the world. Green River country also attracts many hunters, whitewater enthusiasts, backpackers, sightseers, mountain bikers, x-country skiers and all-round nature lovers.

Even the natural history of the Green River corridor is intriguing. Geological formations of all types abound and near-

by is one of the largest deposits of fossils and dinosaur bones found anywhere.

If variety is the spice of the outdoorsman's life, then this river system must be one of the great meccas of the natural world. It's world class fisheries boast six species of trout, something that can be said of few river systems. The cutthroat trout was native but the brown trout, rainbow trout, brook trout, lake trout and even the elusive golden trout have been

A young water ouzel rests on a ponderosa stump after feeding on a midge hatch.

◆

Green River corridor just below Flaming Gorge Dam from the Upper Parking Lot trail.

successfully introduced and are prospering. Grayling inhabit some of the headwater lakes. Largemouth and smallmouth bass are available in Flaming Gorge Reservoir, as are kokanee and catfish. Even a few northern pike exist down around the Colorado, Utah border.

A relatively undisturbed ecosystem exists between the nearby mountains and surrounding high desert country. It is one of the best areas in the West to view free roaming elk populations. Mule deer, black bear, pronghorn antelope, moose, coyote, fox, otter and a variety of other wild critters live here in abundance. It flows through some of the least populated counties in the country.

This edition of the *River Journal* will cover the entire Green River from the continental divide in Wyoming to it's confluence with the Colorado River in Utah, including some tributaries of interest to fly fishers. The natural, fishing and western histories, environmental concerns, trout habits, access, seasons and weather, fishing oriented insects, crustaceans, vertebrates and invertebrates, fly patterns, fishing techniques, area personalities and area contacts will all be included. I've tried to balance this Green River journal between fishing technique, aesthetics, history and area characteristics, with a definite bias toward fly fishing.

Since *River Journal* is fly fishing oriented, I will take extra effort to dwell on the best fishing opportunities and spend less time on areas of limited angling opportunity, while still giving a flavor of the land. Most anglers are interested in the stretch below Flaming Gorge Dam so a large portion of the book will be devoted to it. The fishing techniques described there can be used on the other pieces of water. Naturally, any specialized techniques or fly patterns will be described where appropriate. The book is organized so it can be read straight through or used as a reference for individual sections.

Flaming Gorge Dam
To The Colorado River
(River History)

THE GREEN RIVER FROM FLAMING GORGE DAM in Utah to the Colorado State line is the most popular section of river for anglers. It sometimes sees 150,000+ angler days per year and holds up remarkably well despite the numbers of fishermen. Eighty percent of the fishing pressure is located on the seven miles from the dam to Little Hole. The canyon above Little Hole (formerly Little Brown's Hole) is known as Red Canyon and was named by Major John Wesley Powell's expedition in 1869.

The river currently is one of the best fisheries in the continent and is definitely a world class fishery in every sense of the term. It has a fascinating angling history that aptly illustrates the value of special regulations and informed management.

Flaming Gorge Dam, near the Wyoming State line, was authorized in 1956, begun in 1959 and finished in late 1962. Previously, the river was warm, muddy and supported few if any trout. Squawfish, chubs and suckers, including some varieties

Clear water and the elegant grace of it's trout make the Green River a treasured place and a world-class fishery.

that are unique to this drainage, were the main river inhabitants. Powell's expedition called a species of fish in the river "a queer mongrel of mackerel, sucker and whitefish", and another one "an afflicted cross of whitefish and lake trout". Descriptive terms for fish that are now endangered, protected species. The protected species include the Colorado squawfish, razorback sucker, humpback chub, bonytail chub and roundtail chub. The canyon was regularly ravaged by spring floods that carried huge volumes of silt, sand and rocks, creating rapids and sandy beaches.

When the dam was completed and the water behind the dam began to rise, the once muddy waters cleared of silt and became cooler. The state fish and game officials took quick advantage and stocked brown and rainbow trout. The fishing was very good for a few years but as the waters rose in the reservoir, the water coming from the bottom of the dam began to cool until it was in the 30's and low 40's (fahrenheit), year-round. The growth rate of the trout slowed considerably and fishing suffered. The problem was acknowledged and in 1978 modifications were made on the dam to draw water from various depths of the reservoir. Being able to control the water temperature helped the fishing considerably and it soon became a popular fishing destination.

Still, it was not able to reach it's potential. Over-harvest required massive hatchery stockings and the fishing generally only remained good for a couple weeks after each stocking. Fishery biologists recognized the potential of this huge spring

◆

Flaming Gorge Dam on Flaming Gorge Reservoir creates a giant spring creek-like river that is very productive for fly rodders. This kind of "double" is a common sight in it's trout-rich waters.

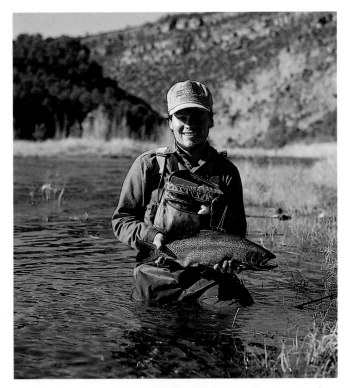

Larger trout move into shoreline dropoffs when the water flows increase. Larry Tullis with a nice trout from the emerging fishery seven or eight years ago.

◆

creek-like river and formulated a plan to improve the overall performance of the fishery by instigating special regulations.

In 1985 the fishing bag limit changed from an eight fish limit to the present slot limit of one fish over 20 inches and two fish under 13 and bait was eliminated. Protecting the 13- to 20-inch fish had an immediate and impressive result. Fishing pressure dropped off to almost nothing because the fish killers could not keep their eight trout anymore and sport anglers had not discovered the changed fishery yet.

With ideal conditions rainbows, cutthroats and browns grew at a staggering one to two inches a month, during prime seasons. Before long fish averaged 13 to 24 inches with a number of even bigger fish. One in ten fish was over 20 inches and a few monsters in the 30 to 36 inch range were available. A fishery like this can not be kept secret for long and by 1987 a number of guide services were operating on the river and articles began appearing in the major fishing publications. Fish surveys during this period reported up to an incredible 22,000 fish per mile, in the first few miles below the dam.

To get a good idea how many fish that is it means that there was an average of more than four fish per linear foot of the river. The Henry's Fork in Idaho averages about 5,500 fish per mile (fpm), the Madison in Montana about 4,500 fpm and even the fabulous Bighorn River topped out at about 10,000 fpm. The only comparisons I can think of would be on the Colorado River below Lake Powell when the fish are concentrated for spawning activity or perhaps in Alaska where the rainbows stack up in certain areas to eat drifting salmon eggs or salmon fry.

By the late 1980's, fishing pressure was intense but everyone seemed to be catching all the fish they wanted. The fishery was holding up extremely well with most anglers practicing catch-and-release fishing. Some fish were proven to have been caught up to 40 times in a year and some were suspected of being caught as many as 80 times yearly—real testament to catch-and-release fishing. In fact, so many fish were being released that the biologists had to recommend less and less stocking because there were so many fish in the river that their growth rate had slowed, with nearly all fish being between the 13 to 20 inch slot limit.

Today there are fewer fish because of reduced stocking but their growth rates are back up and most of the fish are nice, fat and healthy. With fish numbers from 6,000 to 15,000 fpm now, the Green River is still a world class fishery, but the fish do require more finesse to catch. Some anglers quit fishing the Green River because of the numbers of people fishing the river the past few years and others became disillusioned because they were catching fewer fish than before. The fish have been educated.

◆

Dory anglers fishing to bank feeders below Secret Riffle. Presenting the fly to the trout first has advantages and the float is worth the effort, in and of itself.

An angler fishing Two Holes Down just after a spring snow.

◆

The fishery is reaching an equilibrium, balancing numbers of anglers with numbers of fish and numbers of fish with available river resources. Even the fishes' habits have changed to equalize with the skill of anglers. That indicates to me that the fishery is bound to be around for a long time. There have been lots of changes in the river and some are still happening but the future looks very bright. Besides this balance that is being realized, there is now a core of concerned anglers who will see to the future well being of this incredible fishery.

From Flaming Gorge Dam to the Colorado River is about 200 miles but only the first 30 miles below the dam is trout water. From the point where the river enters Colorado State to it's confluence, it's mostly too muddy, warm and silty for trout. If you want a great wilderness scenic float trip, through some spectacular country, you can arrange for raft trips through Gates of Ladore in Dinosaur National Monument, Desolation Canyon or Labyrinth Canyon. They are spectacular side trips but don't bet on doing much fly fishing.

The 30 miles from Flaming Gorge Dam to the Colorado State line is divided roughly into three sections. Section A (as it's referred to by the Forest Service) is from the dam to Little Hole, Section B is from Little Hole to the Taylor's Flat Bridge (in the upper end of Brown's Park) and section C is from Taylor's Flat Bridge to the Colorado State line, near the bottom of Swallow Canyon. Each section has access points by road and each makes a nice day float. As mentioned earlier, section A sees 80% of the fishing pressure because of better trout numbers and easier access. It is also the most scenic section of river.

This rainbow-cutthroat hybrid shows the colors and figure of a healthy Green River trout.

A Remarkable Fishery

THE GREEN RIVER HAS CRYSTAL CLEAR WATER for most of the year. Flaming Gorge Reservoir is nearly 100 miles long and cleans the sediment that comes down feeder streams and the Upper Green River drainage. It collects dissolved nutrients in the lake and gushes out the bottom of the dam as a rich, man-made spring creek. Having such clean, fertile water is bound to increase the overall biomass of a river and the Green is no exception. One study showed over 1000 scuds per square yard of stream bottom! There are nearly that many mayflies and several times that many midges in addition to caddis, craneflies, aquatic redworms and a few stoneflies. As with many tailwater fisheries, there are only a few species of each insect group but what it lacks in diversity it more than makes up for in overall numbers or biomass. There needs to be lots of food to support the fish populations mentioned earlier. Most of the seasonal changes in trout feeding behavior parallels insect movements, hatches and other food sources.

Because of the clear water the trout are very visible. There are few rivers where trout are easier to see than on the Green. On shallow riffles, in big eddy lines, on the bottom of deep, slow runs and even on the edges of rapids, trout can be seen cruising and feeding. Having such a clear view of the trout we fish for has made the transformation of the fishery very interesting and visible.

I first started fishing the Green River in 1977, and have put nearly 1000 days on the river since then. Over the years the fishery and the fish themselves have changed. For a number of years the fishery was supported by massive stockings. It was basically a put and take fishery. There were some wild brown trout in the lower part of the river but the water was too cold for proper fish growth and the hatchery rainbows provided only temporary sport. Only a few fish made it through winter. These holdover trout occasionally got to be very nice size but their growth rate was slow and if they were caught they seldom got released. Even after modifications were made to the dam in 1978, to warm the water, overharvest plagued the rivers potential.

During this time I was learning about fly fishing by testing my skills on visible fish I could see in riffles. I was not a sophisticated fly fisherman but soon learned much about the trout. Stomach pumps had just become available and I used them to see what the few nice trout I was catching were eating. I had fair success on a light brown Woolly Worm and the fish I caught on it usually had a large cranefly larva in it's stomach sample. They also had numerous scuds, mayflies and midges in the samples. I tied imitations of each and my success picked up dramatically.

◆

Spring runoff from small streams flowing into the canyon seldom effects the fishing from Flaming Gorge Dam to Red Creek Rapids -- about 11 miles of river.

The clear waters of the Green allow you to observe the trout's reaction to your flies, which is fascinating and very educational.

◆

During summer I saw trout feeding on large cicadas that landed on the water and imitated them first with black bluegill poppers, then with a foam creation I came up with made from a shower thong. Occasionally trout to six pounds would come up to the crazy bugs.

In 1983 and 1984 there was major flooding in all of Utah and the Green River rose to a thunderous roar. Normal flows regulated by the dam fluctuate between 800 to 4000 cfs (cubic feet per second) but they were replaced with constant flows of 6000 to 10,000 cfs and a high of 13,000 cfs. The lake threatened to spill over the dam itself and plywood shields with braces were constructed to insure that water didn't overflow and erode the face of the dam.

The larger trout didn't seem to mind. There was some great fishing for larger than average fish. Many of the fish were not harvested due to the high water and they grew quickly on the constant supply of food that was washed loose from the streambed. The river was being scoured but it seemed to have a positive effect on the fishery. Fair numbers of 14- to 24-inch fish were being caught. Unfortunately, the word got out and the fish were once again overharvested.

Seeing the rivers potential, fishery biologists suggested that special regulations be implemented, to improve the fishery. They went through and in 1985 the river changed to a slot limit and year-round fishing. The fish soon became numerous because of very limited harvest and they were unsophisticated as well. Only a few people fished the river then so I was often able to have the whole river to myself at times and caught incredible numbers of nice trout. It was a dream stream for me. I began fishing it every week throughout the entire year. In fact I don't think I missed a week in two and a half years.

The trout were everywhere and easy to catch. They ate scuds, cranefly larva, caddis, mayflies and attractor dry flies as well. I had guided on the Henry's Fork in Idaho for two summers and used some of the techniques learned there to really hammer on the fish. Eighty to 120 fish days were common with the fish averaging 11 to 24 inches. My records showed that at least one fish in ten was over 20 inches long, some to 28 inches.

I wrote an article for *Flyfisher* magazine in 1986 because I was afraid that without concerned anglers protecting the river it would go back to the way it was. There was even a lobby of bait anglers that tried very hard to get the river back. The biologists stood firm. Soon, more and more anglers began fishing the Green. Word of mouth and articles authored by various people soon had thousands of anglers coming to the Green River. My little Shangri-la was no more but the fish kept getting bigger and more plentiful so I didn't mind sharing. Professional guide services were popping up to handle the demand. I started guiding the Green River in 1987, for Anglers Inn in Salt Lake City, where I guided for five years.

Over the next few years traffic increased twenty fold. By 1990 there was over 150,000 angler days of fishing on the river every year. The fishing was holding up very well despite the pressure. Fish up to 36 inches were caught and 20-inch fish were common.

The trout responded by getting more selective. They were not the dumb fish of a few years before. Anglers needed to go to finer tippets and smaller flies. The fish were actually getting trained by all the catch-and-releasing being done. There were still so many fish, however, that competition for food helped anyone who did anything right catch large numbers of trout.

There were too many fish in the river and the growth rate of the trout slowed to several inches a year. Fewer fish were stocked and the numbers of fish began dropping.

Today, the numbers of fish have equalized and the fish are educated enough to be a real challenge to the angler. There are still more trout in the Green River than in most world class streams but a few people that were spoiled by the easy fishing of previous years got disillusioned and quit fishing the

◆

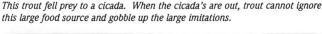

This trout fell prey to a cicada. When the cicada's are out, trout cannot ignore this large food source and gobble up the large imitations.

river. Numbers of anglers are down now and those who know how to fish the river are still catching many trout.

The guides of the Green River have become some of the best I've seen anywhere. Because they were able to see the trout and their reactions to their clients flies and presentations, they quickly adapted to the trouts feeding habits and were able to get clients into lots of great fishing.

One guide, a big guy named Emmett Heath, even got the prestigious Guide of the Year award from *Fly Rod and Reel* magazine. He is known as the "Dean of the Green" and is sort of the informal overseer of the river. His heart is as big as he is and everyone who knows him respects him. He is what might be termed a "guides guide." As might be expected, he is booked solid most of the time. He has lots of stories about the river and having survived the Vietnam conflict, he knows how to appreciate his current, enviable lifestyle with gusto and a sense of humor.

Many guides have come to the Green River but some of the originals are the best because they have seen the transformation of the river and have developed a real understanding of what is going on. Guides like Terry Collier, Mark Forsland, Jeff Cox, Jim French, Dennis Breer, Allen Wooley, Stu Handy, Lysle Waldron, Chris Kunkle, Hank Boem, Mike Sargent and others have become institutions on the river with a following of clients and most have helped develop the fishing methods and fly patterns that are river standards today.

Even with all the changes in the fishery in a short time there are some fishing techniques and types of fly patterns that are standards, but many of the fly patterns change as fish get used to them. Flies like the Chernobal Ant, Peacock Crippler, Tar Baby, Disco Scud and hundreds of other variations have been developed to get the attention of Green River trout. Each guide has his own favorites that he keeps undercover—except for his clients.

◆

Anglers on Kong's Bed, just above Steamboat Rapids. Floating in dories, rafts and kick boats is a popular way to fish this beautiful river corridor.

The trout of the Green River grow fast on it's abundant foods. This deep rainbow fell for an orange scud.

◆

Fishing Techniques And Trout Foods

THE PROPER PRESENTATION AND RIGGING ARE essential for success, as is knowing how to fish through the season as conditions change. Because the fish have been fished over fairly regularly, they have been conditioned to angler's tricks and they can be a challenge. Even though there are thousands of variables that affect how good the fishing is on an individual day, the trout do not have the ability to analyze all that information. When they get selective, people like to refer to them as "smart", to save their bruised ego. In reality, trout only have a brain the size of a pea, but what they do have is the ability to key in on one or two things. To narrow their focus. They block out everything else, which is why fly size can be important but at the same time the trout will completely ignore the big hook sticking out of the fly's belly. If your fly or presentation lacks those certain attributes that particular fish is looking for, your fly will likely be rejected. Being able to see a fish's reaction to your fly or presentation can teach you a lot about trout habits.

The hatches on this stretch of the Green River are not many but they are prolific. The bluewinged olive mayflies that hatch each spring and fall can blanket the water. When these hatches occur nearly every fish in the river rises to the surface to feed. Some large back eddies can have several hundred fish dimpling the surface at once. Fish in the riffles tend to key in on the nymph and emerger stages until the hatch is dwindling, then they move into the slower water to suck in the duns, spinners, cripples and stillborn adults.

The best emergences occur on days when the weather is just a little nasty with a small breeze, clouds and a slow drizzle. On sunny days the hatch may last only an hour or less but there is a large subsurface insect movement which the fish feed on heavily.

It is a favorite time of year for many fly rodders because of the fun generated by so many fish rising or nymphing. The numbers of trout rising may suggest that they would be easy to catch but they are often very selective. With so many insects available they can narrow their focus to one small feeding lane and one stage of insect metamorphosis. The prepared angler will have imitations of the nymph, emerger, dun and an attractor like an olive body parachute pattern. Some anglers like to rig two rods. One with a dry fly and the other with a nymph so they don't have to re-rig for each kind of fishing.

The most effective rig during hatches is the two-fly rig. A good floating dry fly like a parachute pattern is tied to the end of your leader. Another section of lighter tippet material is tied to the bend or eye of the dry fly and a small nymph or emerger is tied to the end. The dropper line can be anywhere from six inches to five feet long. This suspends the nymph or emerger right where the feeders are congregated and gives the fish a choice. They will take either fly and the dry fly often attracts the trout to the nymph. The dry fly becomes the strike indicator and works especially well for any trout feeding within two feet of the surface.

There are hundreds of variations to this rig and all are more effective than the individual flies would be by themselves. If your eyesight is failing, you can still fish size 22 dry flies by placing them behind a larger dry fly, such as a Royal Wulff. Just watch the larger dry fly and if there is a rise about where you think the smaller fly is located, set the hook. You'll be amazed at how effective that is with small patterns.

Later on in the summer cicadas, hoppers and large Royal Wulff's begin to work and a small nymph suspended below them is a very effective double. It is especially effective in riffles and back eddies where insects collect along the scum-lines but will work in any water type. Use your imagination for effective combo's. A Griffith's Gnat with a trailing midge pupa, a cicada with a San Juan Worm, a parachute dry with a pheasant tail nymph and an Elk Hair Caddis with a trailing pupa are all effective. I like to use either an attractor with a small, natural looking nymph or actually imitate two stages of the same insect, an adult and a subsurface or emerger pattern.

There are various hatches that occur year-round and if you want to you can fish dry flies every day of the year. In mid-winter midges hatch even when the air temperature is below zero. Midges can be found hatching almost every day of the year and if fish are rising to a hatch you cannot identify or if you spot trout suspended under the surface feeding, it is likely midges that the trout are feeding on.

After the bluewinged olives (BWO's) hatch, there is a good hatch of pale morning duns (PMD's). See the hatch chart. They can be fished the same way described earlier but with a pale yellow body on the dun.

The caddis on the Green River are sporadic. There have not been big hatches the last few years but they are still important in mid-summer, especially in the evenings, just before and after dark. If caddis are hatching in the evenings, fish caddis larva and pupa patterns during the day. Chamois Caddis and LaFontaine Sparkle Pupas are effective.

Cicadas are one of the unique features of the Green River. Few trout streams have them in the numbers found on the Green. They do not have large emergences every year because there are three species that have staggered broods and three to 17 year life cycles but when they do hatch, watch out. The nymph lives in tree roots (on land) and when they hatch, the

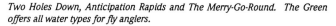

Two Holes Down, Anticipation Rapids and The Merry-Go-Round. The Green offers all water types for fly anglers.

Author Larry Tullis, several years ago, with a four-pound rainbow on the Green River.

◆

adults perch on tree branches and make a shrill squeaky or clicking sound to attract a mate. They are poor fliers and are often blown from the shoreline vegetation onto the water; you can be sure the fish see them. They represent a sizable meal to a trout, one that they cannot ignore. When the fish are feeding on cicadas they can be very stupid but if lots of people are fishing cicada imitations they can become selective. Lots of cicada patterns have been developed but foam body versions, with rubber-legs and elk or white calf tail Trude style wings, seem to be most popular.

When fish are being cicada selective they will often test your nerves. They will rush up to your fly then bump it with their nose, sometimes two or three times. You must wait until you are sure that the fish has the fly in its mouth and has turned down or you will miss most of your hits. It takes nerves of steel and can be quite a humorous experience.

Other trout do what is called a slow roll. They come up under the fly, slowly open their mouth, slowly rise over the fly, with their mouth still open, and roll over and down. Again

your nerves must be solid. The fish does not close its mouth until it has turned back under and if you set the hook during the rise you will miss most of the strikes. A lot of anglers cannot believe this type of feeding activity until they actually see it happen. The fish have seen and been caught on so many cicada patterns that they have learned to test the fly before they actually eat it. That is now true with many other patterns as well.

In most waters where catch-and-release is prevalent trout modify their habits and the angler has to change his techniques and fly patterns to compensate. That is why anglers considered experts a few years ago may have a hard time catching trout now. Trout habits keep changing and they even get used to certain fly patterns and begin rejecting them. These trout habit changes are easy to see on the Green River but they happen in all streams where trout get caught and released regularly.

Mormon crickets also move through the area and land on the water on occasion. They can be as big as your thumb and are a rusty brown color. A clipped deer hair or foam bug with rubber-legs does the trick.

Other terrestrials include beetles and ants. They often get washed off the shoreline when the water level goes up. Fish collect in back eddies and current edges and seem to just love eating these crunchy critters. They are hard to see so you should use them behind the two-fly rig described earlier. When fish are being too selective on a hatch, throw them a terrestrial, it often triggers a positive take. You will need to imitate the hatches but don't be afraid to experiment. The trout of the Green have been known to hit every type of fly at one time or another.

In the fall there are more BWO hatches but they are smaller versions than in spring. Many are size 18 to 26. A friend dubbed it the PMS (pale morning speck) hatch. Light tippets and accurate presentations are required to do well in early fall. If you don't fish small flies you may not do very well.

The exception is when the fish will hit large attractor flies. Medium sized flies are not used much, with the excep-

◆

"I think the mayflies are hatching." Hatches on the Green River may lack diversity but they make up for it in biomass.

Red Canyon anglers try for cruisers in the slow water below Diving Board Rapids. Spot fishing for cruising rainbows, browns, cutthroat and brookies is a fun experience.

tion of stuff like scuds in the spring, cranefly larva, San Juan Worms (aquatic redworm imitation) and egg patterns during spawning activity. The rest of the time you will do best concentrating on size 16 or smaller imitations or large attractors if they apply.

Nymphing is the most consistently productive fishing method on the Green. It has been said that 90% of a trout's diet consists of subsurface foods, which is true during spring through fall. In winter it is more like 98% subsurface. There are insect movements every morning and evening, regardless of hatches. The trout nymph every day even if there are few insects hatching and even when the water is down to 34 degrees. Periods when insects are moving or preparing to hatch obviously are the best times to catch trout on their imitations but trout are opportunistic creatures and will hit nymphs anytime.

Wherever trout get fished over a lot they tend to key on smaller insects which are generally safer because few people fish them properly. The dry fly indicator and nymph system works very well in shallower water but there are many fish that you cannot reach with that method.

The standard method for nymphing the Green is to use a strike indicator, a floating line, a 10 to 15 foot leader and the right amount of weight to keep the fly in the trout's strike zone. The indicator should be placed one to two times the depth of the water from the fly. A small micro split shot should be placed several inches from the fly. If more weight is needed

place a removable size B or BB shot a couple feet from the fly. Putting the large shot too close to the fly will spook trout if its weight is felt and it will spit out the fly before you have a chance to set the hook. If you fish two nymphs at once put the large shot above the dropper.

♦

A little sampling of small Green River nymphs includes the Pheasant Tail Nymph, Larva Lace Midge, Serendipity, Fur Scuds, Chamois Caddis, Palomino Midge, Mayfly Emerger and Floating Nymph. Most nymphs are tied on size 16 or smaller hooks for best results.

This spring screen sample shows some of the trout's "junk food" which includes trout eggs, scuds and cranefly larva and the imitations of each.

◆

insects they also have to increase the number of insects ingested to create the same amount of nutrition. That gives the small nymph fisherman more chances at a trout. Shallow or deep, the trout of the Green respond very well to size 16 or smaller nymphs.

Small pheasant tail nymphs work year-round. One variation, the Flashback nymph, uses pearlescent mylar for the wingcase and it adds just enough flash to catch the fish's eye. Another effective mayfly pattern is the Biot nymph. It uses goose biots dyed brown, gold or black that are wound around the hook as the abdomen of the fly. A little dubbing for the thorax and some flash for the wingcase finishes it off. It creates a realistic nymph that fools selective feeders.

Scuds are a year-round food source and work particularly well in the spring, up to size 12. As the year progresses you have to get smaller and smaller in size. Number 16 to 20 scuds are productive throughout the year. Pink, amber, light olive, orange and gray scuds all work well. A red thread head sometimes makes a difference. Trout will take these small scud patterns as midges, caddis and mayflies too.

When Green River trout are spawning lots of trout are attracted to the spawning areas to feed. They take drifting eggs and nymphs that spawning trout kick up when building nests. Some people don't like to fish over spawning areas but from what I've seen it does little to disturb their activity. When released they go right back to what they were doing when you hooked them. At least 90% of the fish around spawning areas are not spawning anyway. They are attracted by the activity and food, have already finished spawning or are on a pre-spawn feed.

Steve Brayton, the river biologist, says that spawning activity on the Green is not very successful. Immature trout don't make it through the winter very well. Brown trout are exceptions. Since their initial stocking they have been reproducing naturally. They are all wild fish. They have also been increasing in numbers recently which makes most anglers grin.

In any case, the most damage you can do to trout spawning efforts is to wade right through a spawning bed. That crushes numerous eggs and kicks the fish out of their lies. Anytime you see depressions of clean gravel in riffle areas, do not wade on them, they are most likely spawning beds.

Fish egg patterns just like a nymph pattern—dead-drift. The size and color of the egg can make a big difference in success. Trout eggs are five to six mm in diameter but most egg patterns that you buy are twice that big. If you find it hard to tie a Glow Bug that small just cut up some egg yarn and use it like dubbing to create a small, tight ball. Even better is a bead egg pattern. It is a more exact representation of the natural peachy-orange eggs than Glow Bugs and they sink better too.

When eggs have been in the water for a while they bleach out and take on a more peachy-yellow color. When the fish get selective, they can be caught easier on the lighter color.

◆

Angler fishing Little Hole Riffle. The fishing can be quite good for wading and floating anglers alike.

When fry start emerging in spring and early summer, trout feed on these little fish like candy. Drift a small fry pattern in the moderately deep runs below shallow riffles and you can get some good action. Few anglers take advantage.

Streamers are effective at times and places but don't expect to have consistent action on streamers every day. Some days trout will jump all over streamers and other days they ignore or even get spooked by them. You need to experiment and see the trout's reaction. The most productive streamer water is usually the big, moderately deep, fast water stretches that are studded with big rocks. Streamers work almost anytime of year and have accounted for some large fish.

I had a client that cast a large Clouser's Deep Minnow into a run above Diving Board Rapids and had a brown of about 12 pounds follow it and slash at it just at the surface, right next to the drift boat. He didn't hook it and it would not look at the fly again that day. You can't expect streamers to produce lots of fish but you can interest the larger than average trout. Fishing after dark with streamers can be very effective.

When the fish and game people stock the river small fish become prey for the large trout in the river. These large fish usually only have 13- to 14-inch fish to chase and try to eat but when the five- to 11-inch stockers are introduced the big trout go on a feeding bonanza for several days. During this time you can catch many trout on large Woolly Buggers, Clouser's Deep Minnows in appropriate colors, matukas, Muddlers and fry flies. Crazy Charlie bonefish style flies dressed like a young cutthroat or rainbow trout can turn the key on days when the fish are following but not hitting other flies. Use lead eyes so you can hop them along the bottom. Wiggle Bugs work well for browns, especially after dark. Some fish feed only at night and mostly by feel.

To imitate frightened prey, cast to a likely looking run or pocket and strip the streamer fly quite fast at first. Do about three fast strips then hesitate one count. Resume the fast strips. The pause often triggers a take from a pursuing fish. If they are not responding to the fast retrieve, try a weighted fly worked slowly along the bottom. Sight fishing streamers to visible trout can teach you a lot about how fish will respond in areas where the trout are not visible.

If you use a floating line use a weighted fly and a 12-foot leader. Sink tip lines usually produce better. Use a six-foot leader on sinking lines.

Typical tackle for the Green River includes three- to five-weight rods for dry flies and nymphs and six- to eight-weight rods for streamers in 8 1/2 to 9 1/2 foot lengths. Floating lines are sufficient for all fishing except streamers. Here is a list of fly patterns that you might want to carry to the Green River and a hatch chart to let you know when the hatches and other foods occur.

Dry flies: Adams Parachute #18 to #14, Ants #18 to #12, Beetles #16 to #10, Chernobal Ant #6, Cicada # 8 to #6, Cricket #8, Double Humpy #6, Double Ugly #12 to #4, Elk Hair Caddis #18 to #14, Gray Halladay #22 to #16, Griffith's Gnat #22 to #16, Hoppers (Dave's or Henry's Fork) #10 to #4, Humpy #20 to #16, Kings River Caddis #18 to #14, Light Cahill #18 to #16, Mormon Cricket #4, Olive CDC Emerger #20 to #16, Olive No-hackle #24 to #16, Olive Parachute #20 to #14, Olive Variant #20 to #16, Royal Wulff #20 to #8, Rusty Spinner #20 to #16, Thorax Duns (olive & yellow) #22 to #16, Trudes #16 to #6, Yellow CDC Emerger #18 to #16.

Nymphs: Bead Egg Fly (orange, yellow) #10, Biot Nymph #22 to #16, Black Pheasant Tail #16, Chamois Caddis #20 to #14, Cranefly Larva #8 to #2, Flashback Nymph #20 to #16, Fur Nymph #22 to #16, Floating Nymph #20 to #14, Glow Bugs (peach, lt. orange, yellow) #10, Golden Stone #8, Hare's Ear #20 to #16, LaFontaine Sparkle Pupa #18 to #12, Larva Lace Midge (red, olive, yellow, brown) #22 to #16, Midge Larva #22 to #16, Nuclear Roe Bug #12, Olive Emerger #20 to #16, Palomino Midge #22 to #16, Pheasant tail #22 to #16, PMD Nymph #18 to #16, San Juan Worms #10, Scuds (olive, pink, orange, amber, gray) #22 to #12, Serendipity (red, brown, yellow) #22 to #16.

◆

Winter fishing offers a measure of solitude for anglers willing to brave cold weather. This morning began at -20 degrees f. and warmed all the way to +20 degrees. The river water seldom gets below 36 degrees or above 58 degrees and trout are active all winter.

There are rewards for being the first one to Little Hole in the morning.

◆

Late summer and fall sees some of the most challenging fishing of the year. The fish have become re-educated and light tippets, accurate, drag-free presentations and small flies are a must for consistent hookups. Small baetis are hatching, with a large one going only about a size 18. If the selectivity of slow water fish are frustrating you, move into the riffles and use tiny nymphs. If you want to sight fish and test your skills against some of the most selective trout found anywhere, this is the time of year that is most challenging. Weather can be quite nice or not so nice. Prepare for anything.

Browns begin grouping up to spawn in November and are very aggressive throughout fall and winter. Streamers, egg patterns and small nymphs will interest many browns. Fishing pressure drops off by mid-October and by December few anglers visit the Green except on long weekends that offer good weather. The rest of the winter is very lightly fished. Pick a season that suits your style and adapt your fishing techniques to it and you can experience excellent fishing year-round.

Trails and Access

SECTION A HAS TWO ACCESS POINTS. ONE IS from Highway 191, just after it crosses the dam, heading toward Rock Springs. Once across the dam, take the first right, it goes down to the river. This is the starting point for float trips on section A.

The next access point is 8 miles from the dam (7 river miles). Go north from Flaming Gorge Dam about 3 miles. The access road takes off 191 just past the Texaco gas station at the small, government employee community of Dutch John. The road to Little Hole is paved but you need to watch for pot holes and oncoming traffic on the winding road. Little Hole is the launch point for floating section B. The roads can be slick and snowpacked in winter and 4-wheel drive is sometimes needed.

Little Hole To Indian Crossing in Brown's Park is only eight miles by river but the shuttle distance from Little Hole is 40 miles. The distance involved drastically reduces the number of floaters that use section B. There are also fewer fish as you go downstream. It is a good place to get away from the crowds, however.

To get to Browns Park, follow 191 north until you cross into Wyoming. Watch for a road sign indicating the turnoff for Clay Basin/Brown's Park, then turn east. The road will be gravel (or mud if it's wet) the final 25 miles into Brown's Park. Several roads turn off in various directions. Stay on the main road. You'll crest small passes twice, the second marks the steep descent down Jesse Ewing canyon and into Brown's Park. Take this canyon slow and don't try to take a motorhome or large trailer down the 15 degree slope.

The road forks when it reaches the river. The right fork goes to Taylor's Flat Bridge and Indian Crossing, the two take out points if you float section B. The left fork parallels the river to the Colorado State line. Several primitive access roads will take you to the river. Get an area map from the Forest Service in Vernal or Manilla if you plan on traveling the backroads in this area. You can get lost real easy if you don't know where you're going. These backroads require 4-wheel drive during wet weather.

From Flaming Gorge Dam to Little Hole there is an improved foot trail that gives access to this 7 mile stretch. It follows the northwest bank from the boat ramp below the dam to the parking lot at Little Hole. No parking is allowed at the dam boat ramp and no camping is allowed along the river corridor in section A. There are two parking areas above the river, each with a trail to the river. The lower parking lot trail winds about 100 yards down the cliffs to the launch ramp. The upper parking lot trail switchbacks down into the canyon a quarter mile and exits on the river about half a mile below the ramp. Both are steep but improved and afford a great overlook of the river.

The riverside trail is fairly easy walking. Down a couple miles, at Bridge Rapids, there is a wooden, raised bridge that spans the river edge of a cliff, not the river itself. Further down the river the trail takes two short hops over some riverside barriers at Mother-In-Law rapids and Dripping Springs. Toilets are located at the dam launch ramp just below Dripping Spring Rapids and at the Little Hole Parking lot. Others are planned along the river.

No camping is allowed on the parking lot side of Little Hole but you can cross the river in a raft, drift boat or canoe and camp on the far bank. A government campground is also available two miles up from Little Hole on the main access road. There are various designated campsites along the river between Little Hole and Brown's Park. No camping is allowed between Little Hole and the dam. No fires are allowed except in designated fire pits.

Downstream from Little Hole are two foot trails. One follows the river down about a quarter mile to a bluff then zig zags over the hill using old deer trails that have become more defined with human use. This trail comes down to the river about a mile below Little Hole to a flat section of river with rapids at both ends. A trail parallels the river from there.

The other is an old jeep trail that is closed to motorized traffic now. It leaves the north end of the parking area and proceeds up over a hill and down into the Devils Island area. The trail from Little Hole to the Island is about two miles.

From the island an unimproved trail continues downstream another two miles past Washboard Rapids to Red Creek Rapids. The riverside trail ends here due to impassible cliffs. Red Creek is a small side stream that can dump an incredible volume of boulders, gravel and sediment into the river during sporadic floods. Even during moderate runoff it can muddy the river from this point down.

From Indian Crossing boat ramp in Brown's Park there is a primitive trail up the river. It is seldom used because there are fewer trout in this section of the river due to siltation from Red Creek and it also becomes unfishable when flows are up.

From Taylor's Flat Bridge at Bridge Hollow Campground there are short sections up and downstream that can be walked but trails are minimal. From the fork in the road downstream there are several access roads to the river with primitive trails for short distances. See float fishing guide for a more detailed description of river areas.

Float Fishing From The Dam To Little Hole

*F*LOATING SECTION A FROM THE DAM TO LITTLE Hole is a great way to see Red Canyon and get some great fishing along the way. From April through October shuttles can be arranged through Flaming Gorge Flying Service (Dutch John Airport) or Flaming Gorge Lodge. Have them shuttle your car for you or meet the morning shuttle bus at

Little Hole and ride back to the dam (launch your boat first). If the river is crowded try putting in in the afternoon and doing a late float.

You're likely to see people floating down the river in all kinds of watercraft from dories and rafts to canoes and float tubes. The first two are fairly safe. The last two are dangerous. The rapids of the Green River are not extremely dangerous but serious enough that unskilled or unaware floaters can get into trouble fast. The worst culprits are the big rocks in fast water just under or above water level. They often have enough suction or turbulence to flip small craft.

The Forest Service requires that each craft has a bailing device, extra oar and life jacket for each person. Life jackets must be worn by everyone at all times while floating the river. It's also not a bad idea to have a throw rope and first-aid kit along too, just in case.

There are 11 class II-III rapids on the seven mile stretch. The first half mile has some nice riffle water with some fish-packed eddies along the bank. The gravel bars see lots of

◆

Fishing Brown's Park is fun when the water is in good shape. High water and rain can make it unfishable and trout numbers are not large but there is some solitude and a few large trout.

Brown trout on the Green River are beautiful, wild fish that have been expanding in numbers in recent years which puts a grin on the face of all wild trout lovers.

spawning activity in season. Be sure not to wade on spawning beds, your feet can crush hundreds of eggs. There is a long flat section intersected with two nice riffles, the Lunch Counter and Two Holes Down, which always have shallow trout that can be sight fished to. Large back eddies in this area have fish rising almost constantly and an emerger pattern fished with a dry fly as an indicator is super deadly. The dropoffs harbor some large trout.

The first rapids are called Anticipation Rapids and are easy to run through the middle. The big back eddy at the two mile mark is called the Merry-Go-Round. Just below it is Steamboat Rapids. It is a short rapid that has several large rocks placed in the middle of the river. Stay to river right (looking downstream) or you may hit the large rock and flip your craft. It is not hard to miss but capsizes a surprising number of boats, usually rafts full of boy scouts.

There is a big, deep eddy just downstream followed by a productive shelf then a long, slow hole. Watch the scum lines for fish. This deep run has several fish in the 12 to 24 pound range that can be seen when the light is good. They are seldom hooked because they mostly feed on 11- to 14-inch trout and have seen it all. Just above Bridge Rapids is a deep eddy.

Bridge Rapids must be taken on the right side. The rocky reef on the left has been known to eat boats whole. Pull to the far right and be ready to pull away from rocks along shore if the current takes you too close. The six foot drop is more fun than dangerous if you do it right.

Another long, deep hole also holds big fish. It's followed by Rollercoaster Rapids. Rollercoaster is like the name implies, big waves that give you a sporty ride. Take it right down the middle. You can pull over at the bottom and fish shoreline pockets on either side.

Not far below the rapids is a huge eddy known as Lake Bonneville which marks the three mile point. The next piece of riffle water is known as Secret Riffle, but there is no secret about it. This beautiful piece of water holds lots of fish but also lots of people. The canyon is about a thousand feet deep here and very beautiful. The slow water below Secret Riffle has numerous trout that like to suspend just below the surface, especially during hatches.

Diving board rapids comes next. There are several big rocks to watch for. The dropoff at the bottom has a good number of larger trout and the scum lines usually attract more of the trout we affectionately label "scum sucking pigs". If you wonder why it's called Diving Board Rapids, just look up to the left.

Just above the next set of rapids is a gravel bar that sports some nice rainbows and several browns over 10 pounds. They are occasionally seen chasing some poor 14-inch cutthroat trout that is destined for dinner (four mile marker).

Skinnydip Rapids comes next. It has big rocks midstream that require some maneuvering to avoid. Pocket water fishing

Looking upriver, towards Little Hole, shows the gorgeous character of the river, even at high water.

this stretch often produces larger than average hybrids or browns. Back eddies at the bottom are favorite hangouts for trout.

There is a short, deep run and then the river makes a turn to the left into Mother-In-Law Rapids. There are some big rocks midstream to watch out for near the bottom. The current also can push you right into the cliff on the left if you are not paying attention. Small rafts get in trouble here regularly, usually from unskilled handling. There is a great reef and dropoff on the right, just opposite the cliff. Below it is a beautiful sandy beach backed by groves of ponderosa pine and deciduous trees.

The run downstream is swift and just deep enough to prevent wading anywhere but along the banks. The next rapids is Deadman Rapids. It has some rocks to maneuver around, especially the large one at the bottom which is known as Suicide Rock. Uncontrolled rafts frequently hit the rock and can throw you out. Stay just to the right of it for the cleanest passage (five mile point).

Just below Deadman Rapids is a deep, swift run that holds some real pigs. Because of the difficulty of getting your fly down near the bottom, the big fish here seldom get caught but some effort and skill can dredge up some real large trout.

The fast water stretch below is called the Rock Garden. Its full of large rocks and is good for pocket water nymphing and attractor dry fly fishing. This whole area can also be good for an aggressive streamer fisherman.

Dripping Springs Rapid has great waves when the water is up. You can even take a wave over the bow of a dory if you're not careful. At low water take the right or left side because the middle has shallow rocks.

One of the most beautiful runs of the river is located here. The run averages two to six feet deep for 100 yards and trout are spread over the run, behind and in front of submerged rocks. It's a very fun hole when caddis are hatching. Most fly methods work and you can either stalk visible fish on the flats or blind fish the deeper runs.

Can Of Worms is another rapid that has lots of large rocks to avoid and provides good pocket water fishing. It marks the end of the fast water stretch and the point where the canyon begins to open. The runs are full of fish and it's a popular area for wading anglers. The small island on the left is Coney Island.

Immediately below the island and angling down to the right bank is a shallow, rocky reef called Catwalk Shoal. When the water is up you may not even know it's there but during low water flows it creates a small hazard. There are two small gaps, one in the middle and one at the far right end, where you can navigate a drift boat without hitting rocks. It's not dangerous but can ding your boat and ground you. The fishing is often very good here but it can also be crowded.

The long run below gradually gets deeper and slower and is called the Black Lagoon. It shallows out to the boat ramp riffle at Little hole. Little Hole has three ramps. Two at Little Hole riffle and another downstream 100 yards.

Oops! Small watercraft such as canoes and float tubes can be dangerous. The law requires you to always wear life preservers when floating the river, with good reason.

◆

Float Fishing Little Hole to Indian Crossing

*T*HE RIFFLES AROUND LITTLE HOLE PROVIDE LOTS of good fishing but are also fished hard. The first few runs downstream are deep and swift. As you approach cliffs on the left you will also see a big eddy on the right. That is where the opening sequence for the movie "Jeremiah Johnson" was filmed. They actually built a small town there just for that short piece. It also happens to have some nice cruisers in the eddy line.

There is a short rapid with a very deep hole at the bottom. Large fish often lay right where the rapids break over into the deep water. Suspended cruisers are almost always found sipping minute edibles from scum lines in the deep eddies.

The following riffle is broad and shallow on the river's left side. The channel runs along the right side of the river. You can stalk fish on the flats here or fish deep in the channel side. The middle and bottom of this long hole is deep, slow water. Hatches often bring up numerous fish to feed on the surface.

Bootleg Rapids is known for holding some extra large trout. Shoot through the middle. Just downstream to the left are several nice campsites with firepits. The next couple of miles has a series of riffles, runs, holes and one big island that all provide good fishing. Camping streamside is possible at multiple locations.

The large island two miles below Little Hole is floatable on both sides and has good fishing on both. The deep runs below are home to numerous browns and some large hybrids.

As you approach Washboard Rapids there is a grove of large ponderosa pines on the left with a nice campsite. The rapids are long, with lots of pocket water, reminiscent of the

Madison River in Montana. It's fun water for nymphs or dry flies. The long run downstream is known as Pugmire Pocket. Streamers often pick up some nice browns and pods of rising fish can be seen when hatches bring the fish to the surface to feed. Half way down on the right is another camp site that offers some seclusion.

A warning sign on the left bank about three-quarters of the way down Pugmire Pocket informs you that Red Creek Rapids is nearby. These are the most dangerous rapids of the river and extreme caution is advised. The rapids were created by flash floods down Red Creek which piled up tons of boulders and gravel into a gnarled mess of rocks and whitewater. It is always advisable to scout the rapids before attempting to run them. Most folks stop on the left side and walk down to take a look. Camping is available at the head of the rapids and at the bottom.

The middle of the rapids are boulder filled and you can only make a straight shot at high water levels. The right side can be run by experienced oarsmen. You must stay between the center rocks and the cliffs on the right then shoot through a narrow gap between two large rocks. If the water is low don't attempt this run with passengers in the boat. Hit one rock or miss an oar stroke and you can get in trouble fast.

◆

Dory anglers fish the cliffs between Anticipation and Steamboat Rapids.

Deer, elk, moose and many other animals have very healthy populations in the resource rich country surrounding the Green River.

◆

The left side is easier to run since a group of volunteers went in and moved rocks around to clear a channel. If you are unsure about your ability to run the rapids just line the boat through the first 75 yards, which is the worst section.

Red Creek Rapids mark the half way point of the section B float. If it has been raining Red Creek can be muddy enough to turn the rest of the river from here down a rich reddish brown. The silt that comes down this side drainage drastically changes the fishery. The numbers of fish drop considerably and there are fewer hatches.

The lower four miles has lots of quiet water interspaced with some nice riffles and several islands. Even though the fish are fewer, the browns, cutthroats and rainbows that live here can sometimes grow quite large. Since most floaters zip right through the lower part of the float and few bank walking anglers make it here, it is one place where there is a measure of solitude. You can stalk risers or blind fish streamers and large attractor dry flies. Nymphing is seldom productive except for emergers during hatches.

As you conclude the float on section B, the valley opens up even more. You are entering a fun area with a rich history and some different fishing opportunities. There are two places to take out. One is on the left near a large cottonwood tree. The other is downstream a half mile, just above the Taylor Flat Bridge, on the right side of the river.

Between the two ramps is the historic John Jarvie Ranch. He settled the property in 1880, established a store, post office and ferry. He was friends with some of the famous outlaws that used to frequent Brown's Park such as Butch Cassidy, the Sundance Kid, the Wild Bunch, Matt Warner, Isom Dart and Ann Bassett, a lady rustler. Their hideout cabins can still be seen in the hills and an old, underground bar is located in the area.

Brown's Park used to be Brown's Hole until Major Powell re-named it in 1869 to make it sound more sophisticated. Browns Park includes about 30 miles of this remote river valley. Indians, trappers and mountain men used the valley extensively because of the mild winters and abundant game. Brown's Hole was the site of several mountain man rendezvous. The famous adventurer Kit Carson came through in 1829. It was an important fur trading center from 1826 to the 1840's. Brown's Park has lots of stories for an area that even now is relatively remote and with few residents.

Float Fishing From Taylor's Flat To The Colorado Line

FROM TAYLOR FLATS BRIDGE TO THE COLORADO State line (section C) is about 14 miles and contains fewer fish than the other two stretches and is often unfishable due to silt and high water. When the water is low and clear, however, the fishing can be quite fun. Don't plan on getting many fish but there are a few big fish that will take streamers or large attractor dry flies. It's remoteness from the more popular stretches makes it a good place to get away from people for a day. There are several access roads for put in's and take out's making about three different floats possible through this section. Because of the scarcity of fish, if several boats fish through before you, you may not catch any. Plan your float around being the only one on that stretch for best results.

From the bridge downstream, the water is mostly riffles and runs with a few slow pools. The fish seem to congregate around the riffles. You may need to cover some water fishing blind before you find a concentration of fish. The fish are much harder to spot here than in the upper river.

About six miles below Taylor's Flat Bridge is the only serious rapid in the area called Little Swallow Rapids and there is a road to the river at the top of the rapids. The rapids take you through a short section of terraced sandstone cliffs, then the canyon opens up again before going into Swallow Canyon. Swallow Canyon is a deep cut through a mountain about two miles long and mostly slow water. The fishing can be on or off but either way it is an interesting float. As the name implies, mud swallows have built their nests under rock ledges.

The take out is on the left just below where the river exits the canyon, two miles from the Colorado State line. If you keep floating, there is a suspension bridge just over a mile below the state line and a takeout above that on the left. The bridge is called Swinging Bridge and you'll know why if you drive across it's single lane. The road from the bridge is unimproved but passible in a car during good weather.

Below Swinging Bridge few anglers venture because of almost constant turbidity. The river continues into Dinosaur National Monument, where it picks up the muddy Yampa, then goes back into Utah and travels 150 miles before meeting with the Colorado River. The Colorado flows down into Lake Powell, a reservoir known for it's great scenery and fishing for largemouth, smallmouth and stripped bass.

Below the dam on Lake Powell is the famous stretch of tailwater fishing known as the Lee's Ferry section, accessed most often by powerboat. Lee's Ferry area is also the beginning of the Grand Canyon float trips. Lee was an infamous renegade mormon who was known mainly for his ferry and for his part in the Mountain Meadows Massacre in which he got caught up with some agitated Indians and took part in slaying the members of an entire wagon train.

Downstream the river goes through several more impoundments before being diverted into the dry valleys of California. It allows them to grow fields of produce in an area that was previously desert. Most of the mighty Colorado River does not even reach the ocean anymore. It's original delta in Baja California has very little water now. The Green River's waters end up on peoples lawns and in the produce you buy.

There are several side trips that are worth seeing when fishing the Green River. Jones Hole Creek is a fun little fishery. It is a spring creek that flows through a deep red-rock canyon. It's a lush oasis in an otherwise semi-desert location,

◆

Red Creek Rapids is the worst obstacle on the stretch from Little Hole to Indian Crossing. Caution is advised. Scout the rapids first and line the boat through if you're uncomfortable running this kind of water. P.S. There are big browns here.

west of Vernal, Utah. There is a hatchery at the top of the three mile section of pocket water. It's full of six-to 16-inch rainbows and a few browns. The trout like attractor dry flies, stonefly nymphs and San Juan Worms. Jones Hole Creek flows into a remote section of the lower Green River where the river is almost always muddy and few trout exist. Indian petroglyphs dot the canyon walls and it is a peaceful place for a day hike. No camping facilities are available at the trailhead.

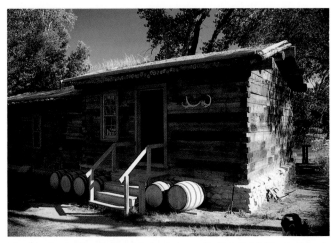

The John Jarvie Historic Ranch is located near Taylor's Flat Bridge in Brown's park. He operated a store that was frequented by Butch Cassidy, Matt Warner and other outlaws and it was a stop on the old stage route.

◆

Strawberry River below Strawberry Reservoir runs through some scenic and remote country and has recently been bought by the Nature Conservancy. It contains browns, rainbows, cutthroats and brookies. The lake itself has some excellent fishing for rainbows and Bear Lake Cutthroat and both places are worth a side trip. Both have special regulations.

Some fun pay-for-fishing ponds are found around the small town of Altamont, Utah, about halfway between the Green River and Provo, Utah. The trout grow large and catch-and-release only fly fishing keeps them there. Rainbows over 10 pounds are possible as are brook trout to four-plus pounds. Contact Anglers Inn or Western Rivers Fly Fishers for booking information.

The eastern slope of the High Uintah Primitive Area borders the Green River Valley. It has abundant lakes, streams and mountains to 13,528 feet high. It is the most prominent east-west mountain range in the United States. It is an older mountain range than the Wind River range and consists of 323,000 acres of National Forest land. It has numerous hiking and horseback trails and fishing for cutthroats, brooks, browns, rainbows, goldens and Montana grayling.

The Green River below Flaming Gorge Dam is one of the best tailwater fisheries in North America. It is also one of the most beautiful. Most of this section is in Forest Service or BLM land so public access is easy and welcomed. It's sculptured, red sandstone cliffs, surrounding high desert and adjacent Uintah Mountain Range make it an ideal place for wildlife. It's a great area to see herds of game, catch some beautiful trout and otherwise interact with nature. It is truly a world class trout stream, with a little magic thrown in. Give it a try.

Resources And Contacts

Following are contacts you might need to plan a trip to the Green River. I've included some government agencies, guide services, lodging and stores.

*Anglers Inn, 2292 So. Highland Dr., Salt Lake City, Utah 84106. Ph. 801-466-3921. Guide service, tackle store, information.
*Ashley National Forest, Flaming Gorge Ranger District, P.O. Box 157, Dutch John, Utah 84023. Maps and National Forest Information.
*Flaming Gorge Flying Service, P.O. Box 368, Dutch John, Utah 84023. Ph. 801-885-3338. Airport, raft rentals, showers, guide service.
*Flaming Gorge Lodge, Dutch John, Utah 84023-9702. Ph. 801-889-3773. Lodging, restaurant, store, raft rentals, guide service.
*Green River Map, AAA Engineering & Drafting, Inc., 1865 South Main Street, S.L.C., Utah 84225. Ph. 801-487-9908. Excellent Green River fishing, floating map.
*Spinner Fall Fly Shop, 1450 Foothill Blvd., S.L.C., Utah 84108. Ph. 801-583-2602. Fly shop, guide service, information.
*Trout Creek Flies, P.O. Box 247, Dutch John, Utah 84023. Ph. 801-889-3735. Green River flies, guide service.
*Utah Wildlife Resources, Flaming Gorge Fishery Investigations, P.O. Box 158, Dutch John, Utah 84023. Fisheries information.
*Western Rivers Flyfisher, 865 E. 900 So., S.L.C., Utah 84105. Ph. 801-521-6424. Guide service, fly shop, Information.

◆

Jones Hole Creek has some rock art in addition to fun pocket water fly fishing for smaller rainbows and browns.

on the eggs, but relax, it is closed to fishing this time of year. Sheep Creek Bay can be good float tubing in spring and fall.

Besides trophy trout and kokanee salmon possibilities that are available, "The Gorge", as it's commonly known, has an excellent smallmouth bass fishery and even some catfish and largemouth bass. Knowing where, when and how to fish this massive lake can make a big difference in success.

Trout From The "Gorge"

*F*OR RAINBOWS, SPRING IS GENERALLY THE BEST time. The rainbows move into shallow, gravel bays and points to spawn and feed. Spawning activity quite often attracts smallmouth bass and the occasional lake trout. Thirty-pound lake trout have been caught by flyrodders from float tubes. The fishing is not always fast but the payoff can be big.

The rainbows like Woolly Buggers in brown or black and will also hit various streamer patterns. The gravel fingers west of Lucerne Marina, Sheep Creek Bay and the area around Antelope Flats are good places to try. If you have a motorboat at your disposal you may want to try where Carter Creek enters the lake.

The cactus blooms of early summer add color to this high desert country.

During years when there are large cicada emergences, the bays around Dutch John Draw have some incredible dry fly fishing on breezy days. Cicadas are lousy fliers and are regularly blown out of the wooded hills and land on the water. When that happens trout and bass go on a feeding spree. These large, black, locust-like insects make a large, high protein meal for trout and they stuff themselves. It's not uncommon to have two- to 10-pound trout slashing the surface when the bugs are available. I even heard of a 28-pound lake trout that was taken on a cicada dry fly from a float tube. Ask around if there are any reports of cicadas out in late May through July, it's worth a try.

Catching lake trout on a fly is a chancy proposition. During summer, most mackinaw live and feed in 50 to 130 feet of water and no fly line will get you that deep. In spring and again in fall lake trout spread out and many cruise the shallower bays. They may only be in the shallows for two or

Jones Hole Creek is a three mile long spring creek and a nice side trip.

Flaming Gorge Reservoir

*T*HIS NEARLY 100 MILE LONG LAKE STRADDLES THE Utah-Wyoming border and has 375 miles of shoreline. It has a maximum depth of 436 feet at full pool and is over a mile high in elevation (6040 feet). This large body of water can be intimidating at first but it has big fish, beautiful scenery and is worth considering. The previous world record brown trout of 33 pounds 10 ounces was caught on the Utah side in 1977. Utah's state record rainbow trout came from the lake also. It was caught by Del Canty from a float tube, with a fly rod. The monster weighed 26 pounds 2 ounces. A new state record lake trout of 51 pounds was recently caught as well. Few waters can boast such impressive figures and it has drawn anglers from all over to sample the trophy fishing possibilities. It is a typical desert canyon, sandstone formation lake with many interesting geological features.

Sheep Creek Canyon is sure to capture your imagination. It's folded, twisted landscape has many beautiful cliffs, pillars and side canyons. It's named for it's population of desert bighorn sheep. Sheep Creek flows through this geological attraction and into Flaming Gorge Reservoir. In September, a large run of kokanee salmon enter the creek to spawn, making it look like an Alaskan stream. Large rainbows follow to feed three weeks and prefer dark, rainy days or even better, night and twilight periods. In fall they spawn on shallow shale shelves, after dark. Two of these places are around Cedar Springs Marina and up by the confluence at Lost Dog camping area. There are undoubtedly many other places but few anglers are dedicated enough to chase these monsters after dark and those that do are quite tight lipped.

Extra large Woolly Buggers and big streamers with trailing stinger hooks are the preferred flies. Large Maribou Muddlers and Wiggle Bugs are also productive at times. There are still some oversized brown trout that can be caught at night as well, although the brown trout population is not what it was in the 1970's. Every year there are some eight to 20 pounders caught.

Flaming Gorge Bass

Indian paintbrush is common along the roads and trails of the Green River area in spring.

◆

IN MY OPINION THE MOST FUN A FLY RODDER can have on Flaming Gorge Reservoir is to go after the smallmouth bass. Their populations have exploded since their introduction a few years ago. There are incredible numbers of eight- to 15-inch smallmouths. Some beauties to four-plus pounds are around. They are widely distributed through the lake now and go nuts on anything that looks vaguely like crayfish, their favorite food.

My best pattern has been a size #8 to #2 Brown Woolly Bugger, with a little crystal flash in the tail. A few areas can be fished from shore but you have a definite advantage from a float tube, pontoon kickboat or bass-type boat. Cast into or along shorelines that have lots of big broken rocks, flooded trees or other structure with a weighted fly. Let it sink some then begin the retrieve. Experiment with depth and retrieve speeds. A fast sinking line or sink-tip fly line is best.

The bigger bass tend to live deeper than the small fish. They also like to cruise around slowly sloping gravel points in five to 20 feet of water. If there are weedbeds adjacent to the gravel bars, all the better. Lead eye flies help imitate the erratic flight of a spooked crayfish. A split shot right at the eye of the fly works just fine too. There is a limit to how deep you can fish for smallmouth bass with a fly and still detect the hits. Sometimes they nearly rip the rod from your hands but more often they just mouth the fly and you need to set the hook on anything spongy feeling.

◆

Flaming Gorge Reservoir is almost 100 miles long and is home for many trophy lake trout, brown trout, rainbow trout and smallmouth bass.

The fish move deep in mid-summer but from late April to early July, the bass are fairly shallow and easy to fish for. It's not uncommon to catch 40 or more bass in a day when conditions are good. Warm evenings often bring bass into shallows along shore and they will hit small bass bugs and poppers fished on the surface. Popper fishing for these feisty fish is a ton of fun but they are not always surface oriented.

When fishing Woolly Buggers for bass you often catch trout or kokanee incidentally. Most of these inshore fish are smaller but an occasional lunker can really put the frosting on the cake.

Sheep Creek Canyon features awesome rock formations and is worth a half day for a side trip. A healthy bighorn sheep population gave this canyon it's name.

◆

Although smallmouth's exist throughout much of the lake now there are several areas that provide consistent action year after year. Down near the dam, in Cedar Springs Bay and Dutch John Hollow, there are quite good numbers and some bass up to three and a half pounds. Since these bays are quite close to the Green River below Flaming Gorge Dam, they make a great side trip and you are not likely to have much competition. The smallmouth bass fishery is actually under-utilized.

Another good area is Spring Creek Bay, just south of the Wyoming State line. Fish the broken rock slopes and gravel points. The bays just north and south of Antelope Flat

Campground have a few large bass. The bays around the Pipeline area have quite a few nice sized bass. This is on the Wyoming side. If you have a Utah fishing license you can get a reciprocal stamp to fish Wyoming and vice versa, so you don't meet two state licenses. The bays around Anvil Point and Squaw Hollow are also good places to try for fat smallmouth.

Big Lake Safety

A word of caution is warranted here. Winds can come up quickly and turn a placid lake into a wind ripped maelstrom. Head to shore or a protected area if the weather cuts loose. Del Canty used to carry a sleeping bag and some food just in case he had to bivouac. He often traveled far from his car, in the middle of the night, even in winter weather. Because he was prepared he never had any major problems. His dedication won him that state record rainbow and also brown trout over 20 pounds.

Another character who gained lots of fame at Flaming Gorge Reservoir was Ray Johnson. He claimed, and probably was right, that he caught more large trout than anyone in the world. Few people could handle his "I'm better than anybody" attitude but his fishing prowess became almost legendary. He was written about in all the large outdoor magazines. He probably caught several hundred trout over 20 pounds from Flaming Gorge by trolling Rapala's on a long line. He was crazy enough to camp in a cave near the lake through the winter just to be close to the big fish areas!

The big brown trout are few now but it is still a world class lake trout fishery. Most of the lake trout anglers troll lead core, wire or downriggers through productive runs. More recently, vertical jigging has become popular. If you have never caught a really big trout, you may want to hire a guide and have him show you how to vertical jig. It is a fun way to spend a day and can be exciting if the fish are feeding. On medium weight spinning tackle you can hook lake trout that average six to 30 pounds. The larger fish often take over a half hour to land. Naturally, you can also split the day between lake trout and smallmouth bass fishing.

Resources And Contacts

*Cedar Springs Marina, P.O. Box 337, Dutch John, Utah 84023. Ph. 801-889-3795. Boat rentals, store, guide service.
*Flaming Gorge Lodge, Greendale U.S. 191, Dutch John, UT 84023. Ph. 801-889-3773. Tackle, restaurant, lodging, information, guide service.
*Lucerne Valley Marina, P.O. Box 356, Manila, UT 84046. Ph. 801-784-3483. Boat rentals, store, guide services, fishing information.
*Roger Schnieder, Biologist, Utah Division Of Wildlife Resources. Ph. 801-885-3164. Information on Flaming Gorge fisheries.
*Utah Smallmouth Association, 3177 Jackson Ave., Ogden, UT 84403. Ph.801-399-5249. Information on Utah's smallmouth fisheries I.E.-Flaming Gorge Reservoir.
*Bill Wengert,Biologist, Wyoming Game and Fish. Ph. 307-875-3223. Information on Flaming Gorge fisheries.

Big Piney
To Green River, Wyoming

THIS STRETCH OF RIVER HAS SOME GOOD FISHING and little fishing pressure due to limited access for wading anglers and high water until mid-July. It can be roughly divided into two sections. Fontenelle Reservoir is located between Green River and Big Piney. Locals refer to the river above the lake as the Upper River and the stretch below, the Lower River.

The river flows through a high plateau that is still relatively unsettled but has historical significance. To the east of Fontenelle about 60 miles is South Pass, an important route for pioneers in wagon trains heading west to Oregon and other locations. The old wagon trails can still be seen. The trail crossed the Green River in several places. The whole area was an important crossroads and meeting place for trappers and mountain men. Authentic reproductions of the rendezvous of years past are still held every year in various locations along the Green River corridor.

Big Piney Area

The river above Big Piney, from Highway 351 upstream to the town of Daniel is all private property and permission to trespass is not freely given. From the highway downstream there are several floats and access points for floaters but if the water is up, there is little water for wading anglers. This section is best floated. The water is flat and often swift but has no rapids between the 351 bridge and Fontenelle Reservoir, a distance of about 40 miles.

The trout are mostly rainbow and browns that average 10 to 18 inches. A few cutthroat and brook trout are also caught. The river is mostly fast and fairly deep water, but there are a few areas to wade, especially when the water gets low in the fall. Access to the river is from several spots along highway 189 and on several BLM roads on the east side of the river. Private property is generally marked, please respect it.

The river becomes fishable in mid-July and is good well into fall when large brown trout migrate up the river from Fontenelle Reservoir to spawn and you have a chance at trout to six pounds and much bigger.

The big fish respond to large streamers and big, rubber-leg nymphs. Other productive patterns include attractor dry flies such as the Royal Wulff, Adams, Parachute Duns, Stimulators Elk Hair Caddis and Griffith's Gnats. Rubber-leg Stones, Prince nymphs, Hare's Ears, San Juan Worms, Chamois Caddis and egg patterns work for nymphers. When no fish are rising, work the runs with a nymph or in the fall, concentrate on streamers.

Several feeder streams in the area are noteworthy. Near the town of Big Piney there are three creeks that flow east into the Green River. North Piney Creek is considered the best fishing. It is a narrow, willow lined creek that has nice cutthroat and rainbows to four pounds. Undercut banks hold trout but must be waded carefully, it can be fairly deep in places. North Piney is subject to special regulations.

Middle Piney is not much of a fishery but Middle Piney Lake, at it's head, is popular with locals. It holds some large lake trout in addition to brook and rainbow trout.

South Piney Creek has a good population of pan-size brook and rainbow trout. You can get to it through national forest land.

La Barge Creek runs through private land in it's lower stretches but upstream in national forest land, fishing can be quite good for pan-size trout. Use your shortest, lightest fly rod for the most fun. There is lots of camping and the stream is easily accessed from the road.

Fontenelle Creek is all private land and permission is needed to fish there.

Fontenelle Reservoir

Fontenelle Reservoir has had it's share of problems in the last few years. It has been drained down to a small pool a number of times to facilitate work on the dam, which incidentally was the same design as Teton Dam that collapsed some years back. The work should be done now and the fishing should improve.

Despite problems Fontenelle has provided some great rainbow and brown trout fishing for float tubers. Lake trout

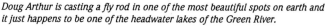

Doug Arthur is casting a fly rod in one of the most beautiful spots on earth and it just happens to be one of the headwater lakes of the Green River.

are also available but generally live deeper than a fly rodder can get. Trout in the two to eight pound range, and occasionally much bigger, can be caught on Woolly Buggers, Byron's Killers, Maribou Muddlers, Dark Spruce streamers, damselfly nymphs, dragonfly nymphs and Black Maribou Leeches.

The lake at full pool is about 20 miles long and 100 feet deep (maximum).

Fontenelle To Flaming Gorge

BELOW FONTENELLE THE CHARACTER OF THE river changes. The current slows and widens, making big sweeping bends to cut gravel banks. There are some good riffles and runs and the water is usually clear until Big Sandy River enters. During runoff periods it muddies the remainder of the river all the way to Flaming Gorge Reservoir. A quarter mile below the dam is an area that has been improved to provide more spawning area. A campground is located two miles below the dam.

During fall the lower river clears and there are trout all the way to the town of Green River but the character is more suitable to the catfish and whitefish that also live just above the lake. The resident fish below the dam are mostly browns and a few rainbow that average 10 to 18 inches. During fall large browns run up the river from Flaming Gorge Reservoir. Even a few large lake trout move up the river to spawn.

Fishing this piece of river can be slow but with the chance of hooking a four- to 20-pound trout, it has a certain appeal. With stabilized flows from the repaired dam and special regulations that exist there now, this piece of river should make a comeback.

Kokanee salmon also move up the river to spawn. The first mile below Fontenelle dam is closed to fishing the last two weeks of October to assure the kokanee spawn is successful. Kokanee are important to the Flaming Gorge fishery.

The stretch has not been very popular in the past but the whole area is set for an expansion of fishing opportunities. It will be a place to watch.

The Green's Headwaters- The Wind River Mountains

BORN OF CATACHYSMIC FORCES DEEP WITHIN the earth's crust, the Wind River Mountains stand as one of the most wild and beautiful mountain ranges in the United states. It's peaks protect glaciers thousands of years

Once the snows melt (around mid-July), hikers and horse packers can travel into the headwaters of the Green River in the Bridger Wilderness Area. It's rugged beauty attracts photographers, climbers and anglers from around the world.

◆

old. The glacial sculpted valleys are studded with pristine lakes and cascading rivulets.

The highest peak in Wyoming is Gannett Peak at 13,785 feet in elevation. It is located on the continental divide in the Wind River Range and it's western slope is the headwaters of the Green River. The Green River proper flows from the north end of the Wind River Mountains, through Green River Lakes and down through the town of Pinedale. In reality, the headwaters of the Green River include several hundred miles of trout streams, about 1300 lakes and many springs and seepages. Most of these are included in the Bridger Wilderness Area which is roadless and covers much of the western face of the Wind River Range.

You can, and some people have, spent an entire lifetime exploring this remote backcountry area. It's peaks are relative-

Island Falls separates a golden trout fishery from it's neighboring lake. The gushing, crystal clear waters of this pristine place can get into your soul.

If you are not physically able to hike the long trails required to access backcountry lakes and streams, or prefer to travel on horseback, there are several good outfitters that cater to anglers. You can book a week long trip, with all services provided or just have them spot pack you into and out of a particular backcountry destination and plan on hiking around on your own from that point.

Golden trout are one of the major draws for anglers. If you have never caught one, you owe it to yourself to make the trek sometime in your life. Their beauty will astound you. Photographs cannot do them justice. They have splashes of bright gold, crimson red, green and purples. They have large, deep black spots on their tails and lower back and they seem bathed in a prismatic iridescence. It may be the incredible colors, the crystal clear waters you catch them from or the majestic and awesome scenery, but golden trout can get under your skin and into your heart. I personally consider a golden, in it's spawning colors, the most beautiful of all trout.

They do not co-exist well with other species and are only found in their true golden trout colors in elevations over 8000 feet. Most golden trout lakes are between 10,000 and 11,500 feet elevation. There are about 40 lakes here that contain goldens. I have fished many of them and have some favorites. They include Faler, Clear, Stonehammer, Peak, Joes, Elbow, Twin, Wall, Nelson, Tommy, Norman, Titcomb, Mistake, Triangle and Surprise lakes. Don't ask me my favorite one, I won't divulge that secret but any of these lakes provide good fishing. The streams that flow into and out of the lakes also provide good fishing. Lake goldens of 15 to 28 inches long are notorious for being difficult to catch. I think large lake goldens are harder to catch than an educated brown of the same size. Stream goldens average six to 14 inches, unless you find spawning lake fish that have moved into the stream. They are usually much easier to catch and often are very brightly colored.

The most effective technique I've found for picky, high elevation fish is to have a 14 to 18 foot long leader on a floating line. A #8 to #16 weighted nymph is attached and cast out in front of a cruising lane in a lake. Let it sink for 30 to 60 seconds while watching for a subtle take. Small strike indicators, that can be stripped through the guides, help considerably. If the fly sinks without being eaten, start a medium-slow retrieve. Make five or six strips, if nothing hits, let it settle and begin the retrieve again. Set the hook on anything, even your imagination.

Lake goldens don't rise consistently, except during a good evening hatch. The bigger fish will take Woolly Buggers and streamers fished deep but nymphs and egg patterns seem to produce best.

Typical high-country fly patterns include Adams, Ants, Beetles, Black Gnats, Dark Spruce Streamers, Elk Hair Caddis, Flashback Pheasant Tails, Gold Ribbed Hares Ears, Griffith's Gnats, Humpies, Irresistables, Muddler Minnows, Parachute Patterns, Peeking Caddis, Prince Nymphs, Rio Grande Kings, roe patterns, Scuds, Siberian Wood Ant, Telico Nymphs, Timberline Emergers, Woolly Buggers, Woolly Worms and Wulffs.

◆

ly new, geologically speaking, and attract mountain climbers, photographers, backpackers and fishermen from all over the world.

The fishing is fair along the major trails and the farther you get away from popular thoroughfares, the better the fishing gets. The remote, high elevation lakes that are nestled between the ranges' spectacular granite cliffs are some of the best places in the world to get a trophy golden trout. The world record of 11 pounds is from one of the headwater lakes. Brook trout, cutthroat trout, rainbow trout, brown trout, lake trout and Montana grayling are found here as well. Each drainage is a new adventure and often holds it's own species of trout.

Getting into the Bridger Wilderness Area is an adventure by itself. It's done by foot and backpack or by pack horses. No roads invade this area, except access roads to the fringes. This is wild and rugged country. Backpacking into these mountains requires that you be in fairly good shape. Many trails are steep and wind for many miles. You must also select and use appropriate equipment.

The cutthroat and brook trout that dominate many high elevation lakes and streams are usually much easier to catch and any medium to small, dry fly or nymph usually does the trick. If larger trout are suspected, try a streamer or Woolly Bugger. Most high elevation trout are in the seven to 15 inch range but certain lakes harbor trout much bigger; 18- to 22-inch trout are considered trophies but a few fish get considerably larger. Because of the short growing season larger trout in high lakes should always be released. It simply takes too long for trout to grow to that size. If you want to eat trout while you are in the hills, find a stream or lake where fish are overpopulated and stunted. These little fish are quite tasty and you'll actually be doing the resource a service.

Special fishing regulations in the high country are almost nonexistent, which is a shame. Fish and game officials state that the reason is because there is not enough enforcement officers to cover that large an area. That is faulty thinking in my book because it automatically assumes that without officers, most people are going to break the law. I don't think that is true anymore and they frankly will never know how good the fishing can get if they never bother with water and species selective regulations.

It doesn't take more than a couple thoughtless horse pack groups or boy scout troops to seriously impact the spawning pool, even if they all obey the present bag limits.

I don't want to imply that the fisheries are depleted because there are many lakes and streams where the fly rodder can do extremely well. Even if the fishing is slow in one lake, you can usually find another close by that has some great fishing and the scenery alone is worth the trip.

Many lakes are so clear that trout can easily be seen from shore. Stalk them as you would spooky bonefish on the flats. If

◆

Glaciers, wind and water have carved these impressive mountains, lakes and streams. This is typical timberline scenery and it changes with every bend in the trail.

they don't see you, you have a good chance to catch them. Fish in lakes cruise shorelines, looking for insects or other prey. It has been said that if you stand in one place long enough you will cast to every fish in the lake. While that is true in some lakes, the fish usually congregate near inlets or outlets.

Larger streams flowing through mountain basins are full of fish, especially sections near lakes where larger fish can move into streams. Most are too high with runoff waters until the middle of July but anytime from then until the snow deepens in fall, the fishing can be excellent. The trout in streams are seldom selective or hard to catch but they are spooky; 50-plus fish days are common, especially if they have not been fished over in a couple days. Sections of stream near campgrounds or trailheads are often fished hard. If you are willing to do some hiking away from main trails, you can be rewarded with solitude, incredible scenery and excellent fly fishing.

There is so much water to fish in the area that the hardest thing to do is to decide where to go. Here is an overview of the waters between the mountains and main river basin. There are several excellent trail guides that discuss the many lakes and drainages in the higher elevations. They are available at outdoor book stores and it's a good idea to consult one when planning a high-country trek. Besides the backcountry waters, many other waters are available to roadside anglers and day hikers.

Pole Creek, located above Half Moon Lake, is a great stretch of fly fishing stream for about 12 Miles. You can catch rainbows, brookies and maybe a golden or two.

Golden trout in their spawning colors just might be the most beautiful of all trouts. Even photographs cannot do them justice because of the overall experience. High mountain beauty, crystal clear waters and solitude combine to make the golden trout angler wax poetic.

The East Fork River, just south of Boulder Lake, has 20 miles of prime fly rod water with its browns and rainbows averaging 12 to 16 inches, very good size for mountain streams. Ask local shops about current access areas.

Boulder Creek, above Boulder Lake, is paralleled by a trail for some distance. The area near the trailhead may or may not have many fish but if you hike in a few miles, the fishing gets better for pansize cutthroat and brookies. The falls and deep green pools are beautiful.

A Colorado cutthroat from the Green River. Trout and the clean waters of the Green seem made for each other.

The streams coming out of the hills can be good. The water is often very cold so dress warm. Lots of private property outside the wilderness area makes local knowledge valuable. Ask around about access points or even better, hire a guide.

The Green River proper begins in two golden trout lakes, Stonehammer and Peak. It flows northwest past the famous Square Top Mountain and on down into Green River Lakes. The fishing is spotty for 12"-20" bows and lakers in the lakes but the scenery is spectacular. You can look over the lakes to Square Top Mountain. Green River Lake Campground is the trailhead for accessing the northern end of the range.

The Green River below Green River Lakes is a nice stream with riffles and deep runs. It's fishable after mid-July but gets very low in fall. Rainbows, brooks and cutthroat trout are mostly small with a few fish to two pounds. A road parallels this entire stretch.

Between Wagon Creek and Kendall Warm Springs, just off the road, is small, shallow Dollar Lake with nice fish to 16 inches. No motors are allowed.

Kendall Warm Springs downstream to Warren Bridge Access Area is a special regulation stretch that has a slot limit. The river can be slippery and there can be lots of pesky flies but fishing is often very good.

Below this point there is much private property and permission to cross is rarely given to anglers. There are some public access points but you may want to hire a local guide who can take you to the best spots and help you with access and float the floatable stretches. The best fishing map I've seen for this area is in Fothergill and Sterlings book *The Wyoming Angling Guide.* Another is the *Wyoming Atlas & Gazetteer.* They detail roads and access points quite well. Check the Wyoming fishing regulations booklet for current regulations.

There are several floatable sections on the Green River here and several others that are impractical because of limited access through large private tracts. The water is very cold most of the year and as a result resident fish are generally not large above the town of Daniel but some larger fish do move up from below. Downstream from Daniel the water is pretty much all private until you get to the upper reaches of the section described in the Big Piney to Fontenelle stretch.

The New Fork River flows out of the mountains through New Fork Lakes and down to the Green River near Big Piney, a distance of about 50 miles. It picks up the East Fork River along the way. The New Fork is one of the top brown trout streams in Wyoming and has a reputation for large fish. As with the Green River, which parallels the course of the New Fork, access is limited and you may want to hire a guide to fish this area the first time.

Floating the New Fork is popular because of limited foot access. Plan on floating about one mile per hour in most stretches. Due to moderately high flows in spring, the best time to fish is from late July through October. Browns and rainbows average 11 to 15 inches and there are a few trout much larger. Small nymphs and dry flies will catch the average fish but try streamers and big nymphs in deeper runs for larger

The Wind River Range is a relatively new mountain range, geologically speaking, and it's rugged beauty is enthralling.

◆

trout. It is a narrow stream near it's head and gradually broadens as it flows downstream towards it's confluence with the Green west of Big Piney.

Duck Creek is a small, meadow stream that winds along highway 187 several miles west of Pinedale. It's a little stream but don't let that fool you. There are some real hogs that live under it's undercut banks. Walk softly so you don't alert the fish to your presence.

The streams flowing out of the Bridger Wilderness area flow through a number of large lakes in the foothills. Most were created when glaciers covered the mountains. The force of the glaciers dug deep into the bedrock. As glaciers retreated,

Fremont lake is a large natural lake at the feet of the Wind River Range. There are 1300 lakes and hundreds of miles of headwater trout streams just waiting for the adventurous angler.

the rocks and boulders it carried were simply dropped and created dams. These lakes offer beautiful camping areas. Most lakes have lodges where boat rentals are available. Many of the trailheads start at these large natural lakes.

Although the lower reaches of many streams in this area flow through private property, the lakes and upper reaches of the streams are generally public lands.

Fremont Lake is the second largest natural lake in Wyoming (Yellowstone Lake is the biggest). It has rainbows, browns, lakers and kokanee. It is 600 feet deep and has 22 miles of shoreline. Try the shallow bays in a float tube, especially early in the season. The inlet can be reached by boat or a steep hike down from Elkhart Park trailhead. Streams above Fremont Lake have great fishing for various trout species 10 to 16 inches long, occasionally larger.

Half Moon Lake lies in a beautiful alpine setting, about eight miles from Pinedale. It's got good fishing for browns, rainbows, cutthroat and lake trout to 16 inches.

Soda Lake is famous for it's large brown and brook trout. It's accessed from a seven mile road from Pinedale. It is an ideal float tubing lake and is very fertile. Scuds and various nymph and streamer patterns work well. Fish the channels between the weeds. Willow Lake is a peaceful lake that contains browns, rainbows and lakers. The access road requires a vehicle with high ground clearance.

If your plans take you on a backcountry hiking trip, outfitting yourself properly is the best way to insure success. If you are not familiar with backpacking equipment, food and techniques, get an appropriate guidebook and study it thoroughly. Carrying heavy or improper gear can ruin a trip for you. Your tent should be under eight pounds, quality construction and preferably a freestanding design. Your sleeping system must be light, warm and reasonably comfortable. Foods should be dehydrated, freeze dried or otherwise moisture free. Every ounce you carry on your back makes a difference. A quality water filter is standard equipment to prevent possible Giardiasis. The pack needs a comfortable hip belt and shoulder straps and your hiking boots should be well broken in and sized to accommodate two pair of socks. You need to be prepared for any kind of weather from 90 degrees and sun to freezing temperatures and snow or rain. You should prepare for the worst but hope for the best. Always carry a quality map and compass in the backcountry. And for heavens sake, don't try to carry a cast iron frying pan!

Angling for high country trout at the headwaters of the Green River rank as some of the most memorable of all my fishing trips. If you get the chance to go, do it! There are so many places to fish that you can just get a map and start exploring. By the time you have to leave, you'll probably already be planning your next trip there.

Resources And Contacts

Here are addresses and phone numbers for your convenience in planning a trip to the headwaters area of the Green River.

*Bridger-Teton National Forest, Pinedale Ranger District, 210 W. Pine St., P.O. Box 220, Pinedale, WY 82941. Ph. 307-367-4326. Area maps and information.
*The Fishing Guide, Dick Miller, Box 555, Pinedale, WY 82941. Ph. 307-367-4760. Fly fishing guide on the Green and New Fork rivers and area lakes.
*The Great Outdoor Shop, Box 787, 332 W. Pine, Pinedale, WY 82941. 307-367-2440. Fishing, backpacking and skiing equipment, trail guides, licenses, maps, float trips etc..

*Pinedale Area Chamber Of Commerce, P.O. Box 176, Pinedale, WY 82941. Ph. 307-367-2242. Contact them for a list of area lodging, outfitters, stores, campgrounds etc..
*Stream Stalker Publishing Co., P.O. Box 1010, Aspen, CO 81612. *The Wyoming Angling Guide*. Fishing guide for Wyoming, with numerous fold-out maps.
*U. S. Geological Survey, Denver Federal Bldg. No. 41, Denver, CO 80225. Topographical maps of Wyoming. Maps for the Wind River Range.
*Wind River Sporting Goods, Box 1360, 234 E. Pine, Pinedale, WY 82941. Ph. 307-367-2419. Orvis Fly Shop, guided float trips, maps, supplies, licenses, info. etc..
*DeLorme Mapping, P.O. Box 298, Freeport, ME 04032. Ph. 207-865-4171. ;2Wyoming Atlas & Gazetteer.;1 Excellent map for exploring Wyoming's waters.
*Wyoming Game & Fish, Box 850, 117 So. Sublette, Pinedale, WY 82941. Ph. 307-367-4358. Acquire local fishing regula-

– Fly Patterns –

Dark Spruce   Fry fly   Glouser's Deep Minnow
Woolly Buggers   Matukas   Optic Marabou Muddler
Tullis Wiggle Bugs   Tullis Wiggle Damsel

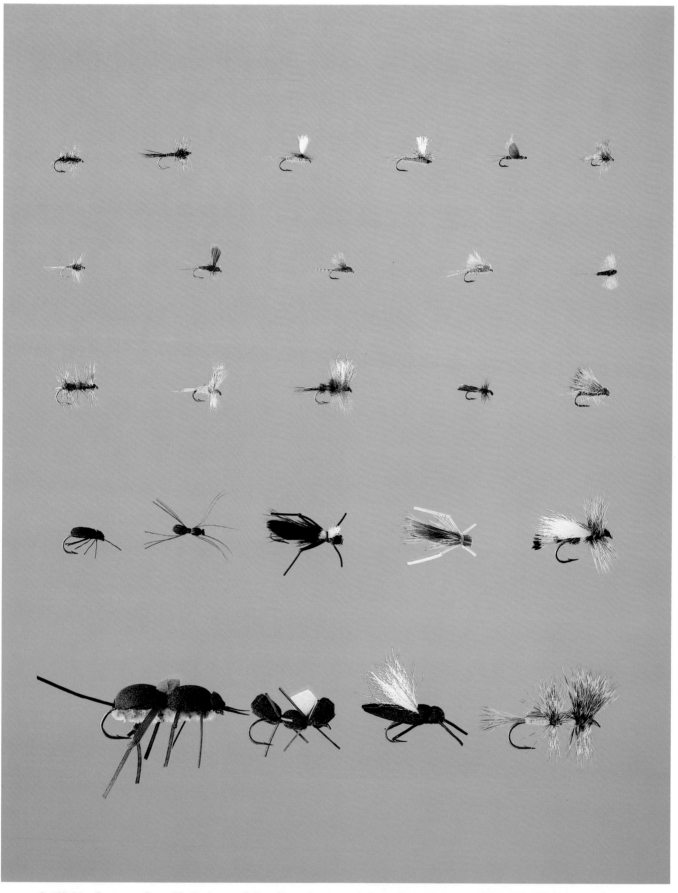

Griffith's Gnat   Gray Halladay   Olive Parachute   Adams Parachute   Olive No-Hackle   Humpy
Olive Variant   Thorax Dun   Olive CDC Emerger   Yellow CDC Emerger   Rusty Spinner
Double Ugly   Light Cahill   Royal Wulff   King River Caddis   Elk Hair Caddis
Beetle   Ant   Cricket   Hover   Trude
Mormon Cricket   Chernobal Ant   Cicada   Double Humpy

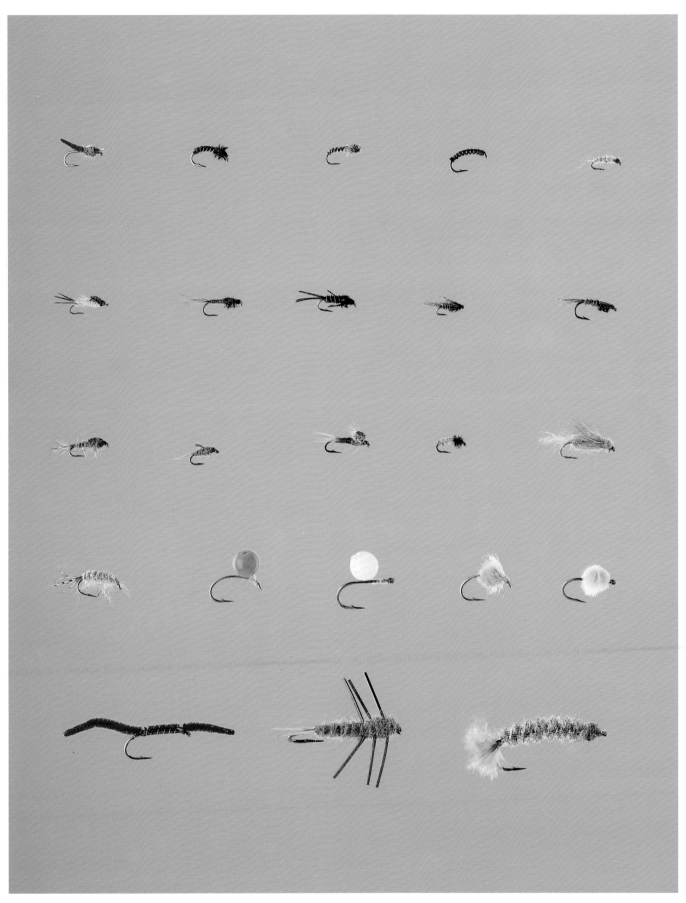

Palomino Midge   Larva Lace Midge   Serendipidy   Midge Larva   Fur Nymph
PMD Nymph   Biot Nymph   Black Pheasant Tail   Pheasant Tail   Flashback Nymph
Hare's Ear   Olive Emerger   Floating Nymph   Chamois Caddis   La Fontaine Sparkle Pupa
Scud   Orange Bead Egg   Yellow Bead Egg   Nuclear Roe Bug   Glow Bug
San Juan Worm   Golden Stone   Cranefly Larva

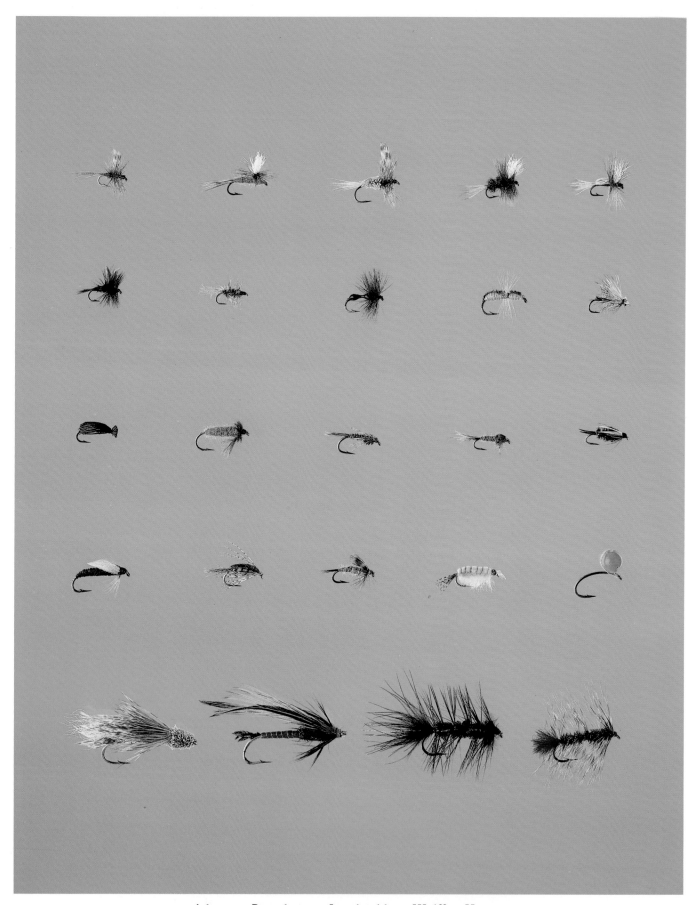

Adams   Parachute   Irresistable   Wulff   Humpy
Black Gnat   Ant   Siberian Weed Ant   Elk Hair Caddis
Beetle   Peeking Caddis   Flashback Pheasant Tail   Gold Ribbed Hares Ear   Prince Nymph
Rio Grande King   Telico Nymph   Timberline Emerger   Scud   Roe
Muddler Minnow   Dark Spruce Streamer   Woolly Bugger   Woolly Worm